V.C.

Everything You Need to Know About

YOUR PARENTS'
DIVORCE

When a parent leaves home, life changes for everyone in the family.

• THE NEED TO KNOW LIBRARY •

Everything You Need to Know About

YOUR PARENTS' DIVORCE

Linda Carlson Johnson

Series Editor: Evan Stark, Ph.D.

THE ROSEN PUBLISHING GROUP, INC.
NEW YORK

Published in 1989 by The Rosen Publishing Group, Inc.
29 East 21st Street, New York City, New York 10010

First Edition
Copyright 1989 by The Rosen Publishing Group, Inc.

Manufactured in the United States of America.

Library of Congress Cataloging-in-Publication Data

Johnson, Linda Carlson, 1949–
    Everything you need to know about your parents' divorce/Linda
Carlson Johnson.
    (The Need to know library)
    Bibliography: p. 61
    Includes index.
    Summary: A guide for teenagers to view divorce as the beginning of
a different kind of family life, to understand what happens to
parents in their lives, and to understand the feelings of everyone
involved.
    ISBN 0-8239-1012-1
    1. Divorce—Juvenile literature. [1. Divorce.] I. Title.
II. Title: Your parents' divorce. III. Series.
HQ814.J57   1989
308.89—dc20
          89-10268
          CIP
          AC

Contents

Introduction

A family begins with a man and a woman who fall in love, then get married and have children. In fairy tales, that is the end of the story. The husband, wife, and children will live happily ever after.

In real life, the story has just begun. Even a husband and wife who love each other and their children very much will have problems to face. Sometimes those problems become too big for the husband and wife to handle. Then their story ends in divorce.

This book is about another story. The story starts after divorce. It is about parents and children. Sometimes they are angry or afraid or sad. Often, they are confused. But the parents still love their children. And the children still love their parents.

If your parents have divorced, your family will never be the same again. Your parents' life together is over. But you do still have a mom and a dad. They still share something very important—you.

Divorce is not the end of family life. It is the beginning of a different kind of family life. This book will help you to understand what has happened in your parents' lives. It may help you to understand their feelings. And to understand your own feelings. Above all, it will help you to know that you are not alone.

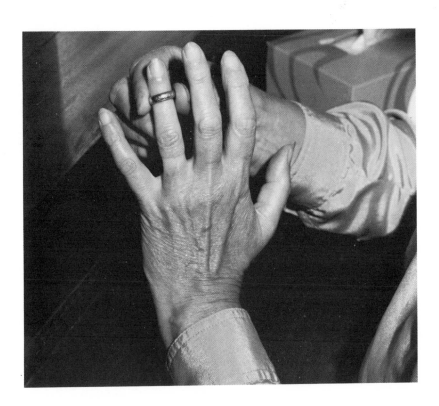

Children sometimes feel that a parent is leaving home because of them.

Chapter 1

I Remember the Day

How do kids know when a divorce is about to happen? Sometimes it is easy for kids to tell. Sometimes it is not so easy. But there is a day when you know. Here is how four kids remember that day.

My brother and I were in the living room. We were watching TV. We heard Mom and Dad yelling in the kitchen. Then we heard a crash. Mom screamed. We ran out to see what had happened. Mom was crying. She looked really scared. Dad was just standing there. He was staring at a huge hole in the wall. When Dad saw us, he screamed, "What are you looking at? Get out!" We ran to the living room. Then we heard the back door slam, and the yelling stopped.

I didn't know anything was wrong. Mom and Dad never had fights like my friends' parents. But one night they came to my room together. They sat down on my bed. They both looked really sad. They told me they didn't love each other anymore. They said they were getting a divorce. Then they both cried and hugged me. They said they still loved me.

I knew my parents weren't happy. They fought all the time. Dad was always saying he was going to leave and never come back. He did go away a few times. But one day, there was a really big fight. Dad packed his suitcase and left. A couple of days later, he came back with a U-Haul. He took a bunch of things from the house.

Mom wasn't usually there when I got home from school. But she was home that day. She was packing up the car. I said, "Mom, where are you going?" She went inside the house with me. She told me she had to go away for a while. She said she had left a note for Dad in the bedroom. Then she left. Later, I found out that she went to live with another guy.

One of these stories may sound just like what happened to you. Or your story might be different. But many other kids have felt the same way you did. Like you, they remember the day they learned

It hurts to find out that parents don't love each other anymore.

their parents were going to get a divorce. It is the kind of day that is very hard to forget.

You may still have bad feelings about that day. If you do, it might help to talk about those feelings with a friend or an adult you trust.

When one parent moves out children have to be more helpful
home.

Chapter 2

Nothing Is the Same!

Sharon is 15 years old. She used to live in a big house on Elm Street with her mom, dad, and two younger sisters. Sharon's dad drove her to high school every day on his way to work. Sharon often stayed after school for soccer practice. Sharon's mom had a part-time job. But she was always home when the girls came home from school.

Three months ago, Sharon's parents were divorced. They sold the house. Now Sharon and her sisters live with their mom in a small apartment. The girls see their dad on Saturdays. He is living in an apartment in a nearby town. Sharon's mother is working full-time. Sharon had to quit the soccer team. She has to take care of her sisters after school.

One day Sharon was crying when her mom came home. Sharon's mom asked her what was wrong. Sharon looked angry. "Nothing is the same!" she screamed. Then she ran to her bedroom.

Sharon is upset. In a very short time, many things in her life have changed. Her dad does not live with the family anymore. Sharon had to move from a big house to a small apartment. She had to quit the soccer team. She has to care for her sisters after school.

If your parents are divorced, there may have been many changes in your life too:

• You probably live with either your mom or your dad most of the time.

A judge may have decided that one of them would have *custody* of you. The parent who has custody takes care of you and gives you a place to live. Sometimes, parents have joint custody of the children. *Joint custody* means that both parents take care of you and make decisions about your life. Even when parents have joint custody, children usually live with one parent most of the time.

• You may miss the parent you don't see as often.

One of your parents may have moved far away. Or one parent may not have many *visitation rights*.

Visitation rights are decided by a judge at the time of divorce. These rights tell parents when and how often they may see their children.

• You may be living in a new place.

You may also be going to a new school. That may mean you have to make new friends.

• It may seem as if your mom and dad have much less money.

Parents who divorce often have less money than they did when they were married. One big reason is that they have to pay for two places to live instead of one. The parent who has custody of you may be getting some money from your other parent. Some of that money may be called *child support*. It is used to help your parent pay for things like your food and clothes.

• You may have to help more at home.

Sharon had to take care of her sisters. Other things you might have to do are taking care of the yard, fixing dinner, or doing other chores around the house.

Sometimes you may feel as Sharon does. You may want to scream because nothing in your life is the same as it was.

It is not wrong to feel the way you do. But you should not keep your feelings inside until you *do* scream. You should talk to your mom or dad about your feelings. They may not know how upset you are. You could also share your feelings with friends. You may want to talk with your school counselor or a teacher. If you go to a church or synagogue, you may want to talk with someone there.

Talking to people won't change what has happened to you. But it may help just to share your problems. It may also help to know that there are other people who care enough about you to listen.

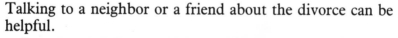
Talking to a neighbor or a friend about the divorce can be helpful.

Chapter 3

Who's To Blame?

*T*om asks his mom for money for a new jean jacket. She says, "Forget it! I'm broke. Maybe if your father hadn't walked out on us, we would have the money."

Sara walks in the house, but her mother doesn't hear her. She is sitting at the kitchen table talking to her friend Joan. Joan says, "You didn't do anything wrong. You did everything for him. And what does he do to thank you? He just walks out. If you ask me, he was never good enough for you."

Bill is staying with his grandparents for a week. He hears them talking in the living room when they think he is asleep. "It's such a shame," his grandmother says. His grandfather says, "Yes, it's that wife of his. If she had not run around the way she did, they might still be together."

17

Tom, Sara, and Bill all have the same problem. People around them are angry. Often, when people are angry, they are feeling pain. And they want to find someone to blame for their pain.

If your parents are divorced, you may have heard your mother or father blame each other for the divorce. Or you may have heard someone else talking about who was to blame.

It is hard not to listen, especially when it's your own mom or dad talking. But listening to these angry voices will just make you angry too.

If you are angry about a divorce, it can eat you up inside. And it may make it hard to be around your mom or dad.

Remember, divorce is almost never one person's fault. But when a divorce happens, people often look for someone to blame.

If you can, you should try not to blame anyone. What happened is in the past. Now your mom and dad are both feeling the pain of divorce. They need your love more than ever now. And you need their love too.

But what if you *do* think someone is to blame? It won't help anyone if you stay angry. You should try to forgive. That isn't easy. But it is important. Once you forgive, you can stop being angry. Then you will feel better about your parent—and yourself.

Children can be upset if grandparents take sides when parents argue.

If you feel angry all the time about a divorce,
you need help. You should talk to someone you
trust. The person you choose should not be angry
about the divorce. You might try to talk to a school
guidance counselor or someone at your church or
synagogue.

You will need to set up a time to see one of these
people. That may mean talking to the person's
secretary. You don't have to tell the secretary all
about your problem. You can just say, "I would
like to talk to . . . . Could you tell me when I
might be able to do that?"

The secretary may ask what you want to talk
about. You could say that you want to talk about
your parents' divorce. But what if you don't want
to talk about your problem? Say so, but don't act
angry at the secretary. Instead, just say, "I'd rather
not talk about it. It's a personal problem. But it is
important."

If you do set up a time to see someone, go to
the meeting. Tell the person how you are feeling.
Remember, it is important not to keep your
feelings inside.

**If you feel angry all the time about a divorce,
you need help.**

Chapter 4

It's Not Your Fault

Many kids don't blame their mother or father for a divorce. They blame themselves. Dwayne, Rae Ann, and Jennifer are three kids who think they caused their parents to break up.

○ Dwayne is 16. He remembers what things were like before the divorce. His parents fought all the time. Most of the fights were about him. He was always in trouble.

○ Rae Ann is 14. She always fought with her sister Stacey. Her dad would blow up just about every night. He would say, "I work all day and I come home to this? I should have stayed at work!"

○ Jennifer is 13. Her mom said she and Jennifer's dad were happy once. She said everything changed when the kids came along.

Sometimes children think that a parent leaves home because they made the parent angry.

These kids blame themselves for different reasons. Dwayne saw his parents fighting about him all the time. He thought those fights caused the divorce. Rae Ann knew her fights with her sister made her father angry. She thought that if she hadn't been so bad, her father might have stayed. Jennifer didn't know what she had done. She just knew her mom seemed unhappy to have kids. Jennifer wished she had never been born.

What did these kids do about their feelings?

○ Dwayne became very angry with himself. He took his anger out on everyone and everything around him. He got in fights all the time. He drank. He took drugs. He wouldn't do anything his mother said. He got drunk and wrecked his father's car.

○ Rae Ann and her sister visited her father every weekend. Rae Ann never said anything. She was afraid she would start fighting with Stacey. Rae Ann's dad couldn't understand what was wrong.

○ Jennifer got very depressed. She felt sick all the time. She stopped talking to her friends. One day, she tried to kill herself. She took as many pills as she could find. Her mom found her lying on the bedroom floor. She rushed Jennifer to the hospital. Jennifer had to have her stomach pumped out. When Jennifer woke up, she cried. She said she wished she had died.

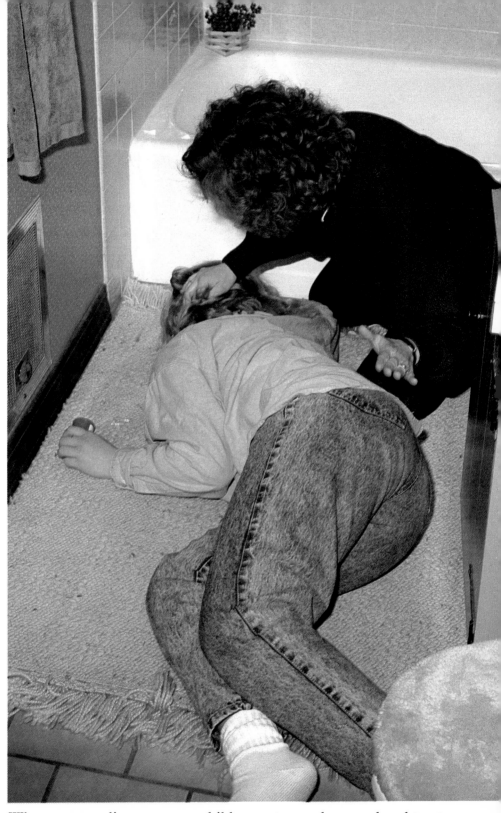

When parents divorce, some children get very depressed and try to commit suicide.

None of these kids caused their parents to split
up. But they thought they did. They became
angry, afraid, and sad. They couldn't go on with
their lives until they got help. All three did get
help.

○ Dwayne had to go to a special school for
troubled kids. The counselors there helped him
with his drinking and drug problems. They
found out how Dwayne felt about his parents'
divorce. Then the counselors talked to Dwayne
and his parents. Dwayne learned the divorce was
not his fault. Dwayne's parents learned about
ways to help Dwayne.

○ Rae Ann finally talked to her dad about what
was bothering her. He told her that the divorce
wasn't her fault at all. Then Rae Ann wasn't
afraid to talk to Stacey when their dad was
around.

○ Jennifer's mom told her more about the divorce.
Jennifer found out there were many reasons for
the divorce. Jennifer's mom and dad both told
her how much they loved her. They made sure
she knew the divorce was not her fault. They
began spending more time with Jennifer and her
brothers.

Do you blame yourself for your parents' divorce? You may think you did something to make the divorce happen. Or you may just feel angry or sad all the time.

It is important to remember that your parents' divorce is not your fault. Your parents may have said things they didn't really mean. They may have fought about you. They may have been angry with you. But divorce is not between parents and children. It is between a husband and wife.

If you blame yourself for your parents' divorce, don't keep your feelings inside. If you can talk to your mom or dad, do that.

Tell your mom or dad how you are feeling. You might say, "Dad (or Mom), there's something that has been bothering me." You might say, "Mom (or Dad), I've been feeling very upset ever since the divorce. But I'm not upset with you. I'm upset with me."

Then you should tell your mom or dad that you blame yourself for the divorce. Try to tell your mom or dad exactly why you feel this way.

Most of the time, talking to your parents is the best thing to do. But that may be too hard for you to do. If it is, talk to another adult you trust. Do not keep your feelings to yourself.

Sometimes divorced parents try to buy a child's love with presents.

Chapter 5

Don't Take Sides!

After a divorce, parents must start new lives apart. But they still share children. So the parents must see and talk with each other.

Sometimes, parents are still friends after their divorce. They talk to each other about their kids. They set rules for their kids to follow in mom's house and dad's house. They agree not to say bad things about each other to their kids.

But sometimes, divorced parents are not friendly to each other. They are still angry. They may not talk to each other very much. But they do talk to their kids. These parents say bad things about each other. They try to get the kids to agree with those things. Kids may feel they are in the middle of a tug-of-war between their mother and father.

Sometimes parents try to get their kids to take sides for another reason. They are afraid of losing their kids' love. Then parents may try to do things to "buy" love. They may take their kids to special places. They may buy them very expensive things. Or they may let their kids do whatever they want to do.

When one parent does these things, the other parent may be very upset. Again, the kids are in the middle of a tug-of-war.

What should you do if your parent tries to get you to take sides?

○ If your parents say bad things about each other, tell them you don't want to hear those things. You might say, "I know how you feel. But please don't talk that way any more. I still love my dad (or mom)."

○ If one parent tries to "buy" your love, be careful. You might feel good about getting presents or going to special places. But don't be fooled. These things are not what love is about. You should also let your other parent know that you love him or her.

The most important thing to remember is: Don't take sides. You need both of your parents' love to help you through this hard time. And to help you grow up happy and strong. Let them know that.

Special Cases

Sometimes, parents may do things that are harmful to themselves or someone else. Then you may have to stay away from them until they get help. Or you may have to tell someone what they are doing so they can get help. Here are some of the things a parent might do.

• **Get drunk or high on drugs all the time.** If your parent has a drinking or drug problem, you won't be able to help. Talk to an adult you trust about the problem.

• **Become violent.** If your parent tries to hurt you or your other parent, you should call the police. They are trained to help.

• **Act very depressed.** After a divorce, parents can be very upset. That's normal. But sometimes a mom or dad may seem to want to die. If one of your parents talks about suicide, tell another adult.

An unhappy parent might become violent.

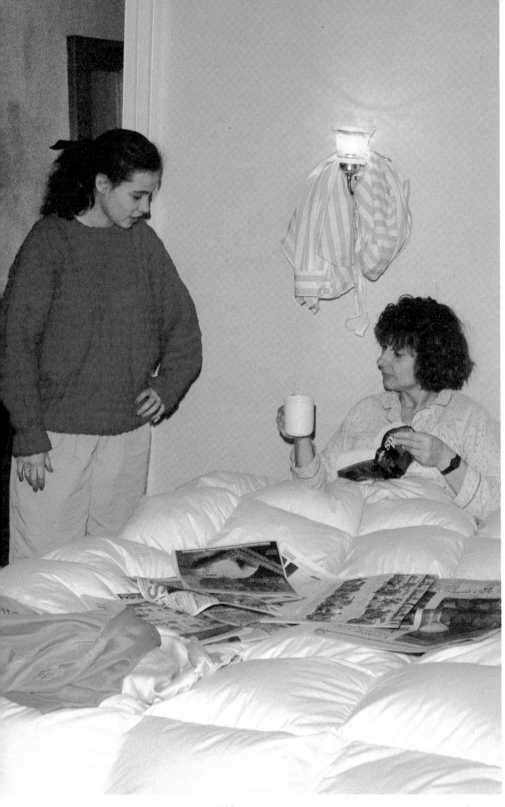

Helping a parent through difficult times can be an extra burden for young people.

Chapter 6

When Parents Act Like Children

*T*om calls Sue for a date on Saturday night. Sue turns him down. She says she has to stay home because her mother needs her.

Eric visits his dad on weekends. His dad always takes him out to bars with him. Eric's dad usually gets drunk. Eric has to drive him home. Then Eric helps his dad undress and puts him to bed.

Sharnelle can't go anywhere anymore. When she comes home, the house is a mess. Her mother is always curled up in her bedroom with a book. Sharnelle has to do all the cleaning and cooking.

The parents of these kids are acting like children. They don't want to face their lives alone. Sue's mom is afraid to be alone. Eric's dad expects Eric to take care of him. Sharnelle's mom doesn't want to act like an adult anymore. She wants to stay in her room.

When parents act like children, children often have to act like parents. But sometimes this goes too far. Then the children don't have lives of their own anymore.

What should you do if this happens to you? First, you should try to talk to the parent who is causing the problem for you. When you do, try not to sound too angry. Your parent may listen better if you are calm. Here is how this talk might go for Sue, Eric and Sharnelle.

○ Sue might say, "Mom, I really miss my friends. I would like to go out this Saturday night. I know you don't like to be alone. Is there someone else you could ask to come over?"

○ Eric might say, "Dad, I love you but I'm worried about you. You seem to be drinking more and more. That makes me scared. I wish you would stop. Maybe we could go to a movie instead of to a bar next weekend."

It is important for children to communicate with their divorced parents.

○ Sharnelle might say, "Mom, I'm tired. I understand that you are sad. But I can't handle my schoolwork and all the housework too. Could you help me with dinner tonight?"

If this talk doesn't help, you might need to go to someone else. Try talking to another adult in the family who you think might understand. Call your clergyman or school guidance counselor. These people might be able to help. They may help you find ways to talk to your parents. They may even talk to your parents for you. If you *don't* want them to do that, you should say so.

Being separated from the family can create feelings of guilt.

Chapter 7

Loving Both Parents

Sometimes it's hard to love your parents. Even when parents are together, that can be true. But when parents are apart, it's even harder to love them both. But it is important that you try.

When parents divorce, kids usually feel very bad. But they don't feel *as* bad when they know they are loved by both parents.

You may be feeling very confused about what has happened between your parents. You may even be angry at one of them. But try to remember what parents often say to children who do bad things. "I am angry about what you have done. But I still love *you*." You may be angry with your parents. But you still need to love *them*.

37

Your parents may not make it easy to love them. Let's say that you are living with your mom. She is still hurting from the divorce. She snaps at you all the time for no reason. She doesn't seem to hear what you say. She orders you around all the time.

If your mom acts like this, you might feel that you want to get away from her. But believe it or not, your mom needs you. Try to be patient with her. Try not to get too angry yourself. Try to show her in small ways that you love her. Remember, you have only one mother.

You may have to try even harder with the parent who is living away from home. Usually, this parent is the dad. His life has changed completely. He is probably in pain too. He feels just as bad about the divorce as your mom does. But he may feel he has lost his children too. You may be angry at him for leaving you. Still, you should try to reach out to him. That may not be easy. It may take a long time. But it is important for both of you. Remember, you have only one father.

**You may be angry at him for leaving you.
Still you should try to reach out to him.**

Chapter 8

Why Can't They Get Back Together?

*I*t had been a year since Heather's parents divorced. Her mom and dad seemed to get along so well. They talked on the phone all the time. When Dad came to pick Heather up, Mom always met him at the door. They seemed happy to see each other, and they always talked for a while. Once, Mom even asked Dad in for coffee.

After the divorce, Sam went to live with his father. He really missed his mom. He talked all the time about things they had done together as a family. Dad listened, but he didn't say anything.

Jason hasn't talked to his father since the divorce. It has been six months. Jason made a promise to himself. He would not talk to his dad until his dad came back home for good.

Heather, Sam, and Jason love their parents. They are like many kids who want their parents to get back together. They don't understand why their parents got a divorce. Even if they do know why, they choose not to remember. Instead, they think of the good times they had as a family. They think all their problems would be over if only their mom and dad would get back together.

You may sometimes feel this way. Your feelings are natural. You want the people you love most to live with you. But it is important for you to understand that your mom and dad probably will not get back together.

Try to think about what happened before the divorce. Was everything really so good? You may remember fights and angry words. Or maybe you don't. Sometimes parents don't show their problems to their kids. Then it may be harder for the kids to understand when parents split up.

You may not understand completely why your parents divorced. As time goes on, they may talk more about it to you. But keep in mind that talking about what happened won't change anything. And keep in mind that it is not up to you to get your parents back together.

Remember that you were not to blame for the divorce. It didn't happen because of something you did. You can't make your parents get back together either. If they do get back together, it won't be because of something you do.

A family can still get along together, even if the parents are divorced.

You need to accept that your parents are divorced. Once you do, you can start making things work just the way they are. You can enjoy the time you have with your mom and with your dad. You can start living in the present instead of the past.

It is not unusual to feel alone and confused after a divorce.

Chapter 9

You're Not Alone

*J*uan *used to have a lot of friends. He was on the basketball team. He got good grades. He always had a smile for everyone. Then Juan's parents got a divorce. Juan was out of school often. He walked with his head down. He quit the basketball team. He started to get into fights. At first, his friends called him every night. Juan wouldn't even come to the phone. After a while, they stopped calling.*

Juan feels as if no one else understands his problems. He thinks no one has ever felt as bad as he feels now. He doesn't think he will ever be happy again. He feels very much alone.

You may feel alone too. But you are not. About three out of every ten kids have been through a divorce. That means that in a class of 30 kids, 9 of them probably have divorced parents. Some live with just their mom or dad. Some live with a stepparent too.

Talking to someone who has been through a divorce may help you feel better. If none of your friends have divorced parents, talk to your school counselor. He or she may know of a *support group* that can help you. A support group is a group of people who get together to talk about their problems. They help, or support, each other.

Other friends may help too. If you have a best friend, you should talk to him or her. Sometimes it helps just to have someone who will listen.

It is also important to keep busy. Try not to think about your problems all the time. Instead, go to that basketball practice. Do your homework. Go out with your friends. Doing these things won't solve your problems. But at least you can keep them out of your mind for a while.

If you still feel down, tell your mom or dad or someone else you trust. Remember, you do not have to be alone.

Chapter **10**

When Parents Date

*J*ohn's mother walked into the living room in a new *dress. She was all made up and was wearing perfume.*

"How do I look?" she asked John.

"Where are you going?" John asked.

"Out with a man I met at work. So how do I look?" his mom asked again.

"Does Dad know about this?" John asked.

"No, of course not. John, your dad and I have been divorced for six months." His mom sounded frustrated.

"Yeah, I know, but . . ." John started to say.

"But I shouldn't date?" his mom interrupted.

"Oh, do whatever you want." John was almost yelling. He stomped up the stairs.

"John," his mother called after him. John's answer was to slam his door.

John is 15. He is very upset with his mother. He doesn't really even understand why. But he feels that his mother is cheating on his father.

John's mother isn't doing that. She is a single woman, and she felt attracted to a man. She decided to go out with him. But John has a hard time understanding why his mother wants to do that. He hasn't really accepted that his parents are divorced.

Shana's dad said he had to talk with her about something. He said he was going out with a woman on Friday night.

"How old is she?" Shana asked.

"Is that important?" her dad asked.

"Yes," Shana said.

"She's 28," her dad said.

"Twenty-eight? She's ten years younger than Mom! What does she look like?" Shana said.

"She's nice looking," her dad said.

"Is she prettier than Mom?" Shana asked.

"I wouldn't compare them," Shana's dad answered.

"Are you going to sleep with her?" Shana asked.

"Shana!" Her dad sounded shocked. "Why would you say a thing like that?"

Shana started to cry.

Shana is 14. Her dad's date has upset her. She feels that her dad is not just her dad any more. He

A child may object to a parent dating and meeting new partners.

is a man who goes out with women. Shana herself is becoming a woman. She knows what it is like to feel attracted to a boy. It is hard for her to think about her dad having feelings like that for a woman. It is especially hard for her to think about her dad being with a woman other than her mom. Shana also feels very close to her dad. She feels that this young, attractive woman may take her dad away from her.

Shana is very confused. In one way, she understands her father's need to date. But in another way, she is angry about it. And she is afraid too.

If your divorced parents are dating, you may feel some of the things John and Shana felt. It's not easy to see your mom and dad as single people. But that's what they are. They are trying to start new lives. That means they will make new friends. And they will probably date.

When that happens, you may be confused or upset. If you are, there are a few things you should *not* do.

○ You should not yell at your mom or dad. If you do, your mom or dad may scream right back at you. Then no one will feel any better.

○ You should not tell your mom or dad what to do either. If you do, they may tell you to stay out of their personal lives. You will still feel bad, but you won't be able to talk to your parents about your feelings.

○ You should not talk about your feelings in front of your mom's or dad's date. You may make the date feel very upset. And you may make your mom or dad angry.

What *should* you do about your feelings? Talk to your mom or dad. When you do, try to stay calm. It's okay to say that you are upset. But try not to *act* upset. You might say, "I know you are single now. But it really bothers me to see you with someone besides Mom (or Dad). I don't know why I feel this way, but I do."

Even if you are calm, your mom or dad may become angry. If that happens, say, "Maybe we shouldn't talk about this right now."

Talking this way to your mom or dad may be hard. It's especially hard if you and your parents often yell at each other. But it is best to stay calm. If *you* do, there is a better chance that your parents will stay calm too.

It may be difficult for a son or daughter to accept a new family member.

Chapter **11**

When Parents Remarry

One day, your mom or dad may decide to marry again. That day could come very soon. Or it may never come at all. If that day does come, it will be an important day for you too. It will mean big changes in your life. Here are five stories about kids whose parents decided to marry again.

Seth is very troubled. He hasn't had much time to understand his parents' divorce. Now he has to get used to a stepfather too.

Seth's mom was divorced one week and married the next. Seth knew that would happen. His mom had left his dad because of Jerry. But it all seemed to happen so fast. His mom and Jerry went away together for a week, then they came home.

Jerry told Seth he wouldn't try to replace Seth's
father. But in just a few days, Jerry was telling
Seth what to do. Seth wanted to leave home, but
he couldn't. He was only 14. He called his dad and
asked if he could stay with him. But Seth's dad
said he couldn't afford an apartment big enough for
the two of them.

*Janice didn't mind it that her mom dated. At least,
not until Chuck came along.*

Janice's mom had been dating for a year. But in
all that time, she had not brought her dates home.
She always met her date at a restaurant. Then one
night Janice's mom invited a man named Chuck to
dinner. She and Chuck told Janice that they were
going to be married.
Later that night, Janice's mom asked Janice if
she liked Chuck. Janice didn't like him at all. He
wasn't at all like her dad. He laughed too loud,
and he swore all the time. But Janice didn't tell her
mother how she felt. Her mother seemed so happy.

*Justine was happy when her dad married Esther.
But then Esther and her two boys moved in.*

Justine liked Esther all right. That wasn't the
problem. It was Esther's two stupid sons that drove
Justine crazy. They were 9 and 11 years old and
nothing but trouble.

Justine's dad said she should give the boys a chance. She tried. But the boys didn't try back. They called her a pig, and they said rotten things about her boyfriend. Justine hated them so much that she began to hate Esther too. Then she even began to hate her dad for marrying Esther.

Joe and his dad had never been very close. So Joe was happy when Stu came into his mother's life.

Joe liked Stu from the first time they met. That was about a year after the divorce. Stu took Joe and Joe's mom to a hockey game. They had a great time together. When Stu came over to the house, he always had time for Joe. They played catch in the yard. Sometimes they just sat on the porch and talked. So Joe was very happy when his mom and Stu got married.

Sherry didn't know that when her dad remarried, she would feel so left out.

Sherry lived with her mom during the week and her dad on weekends. Sherry and her dad always had a great time. But then Sherry's dad married Kathryn. Sherry didn't feel wanted at her dad's house anymore. Every weekend that she visited was worse.

At first, Kathryn just gave Sherry dirty looks when Sherry's dad wasn't watching. Then Kathryn started to boss Sherry around. She told Sherry that she should learn some manners. Every time Sherry touched anything in the house, Kathryn yelled at her.

Sherry tried to talk to her dad about Kathryn. But her dad wouldn't listen. He kept taking Kathryn's side. Sherry started finding reasons to stay with her mom on weekends.

For Sherry, her dad's marriage is terrible. Sherry feels as if she has lost her dad—again. She is glad she gets along really well with her mom. For Joe, his mom's marriage is great. He feels as if he has found a dad—at last. Quite often, things turn out this way. Seth, Janice, and Justine aren't very happy with what has happened in their parents' lives. But in time, things may get better for them.

Each of these kids' stories is special. If your mom or dad decides to remarry, another special story will begin. That story will be yours.

For Sherry, her dad's marriage is terrible. Sherry feels as if she has lost her dad—again.

Chapter 12

Life After Divorce

There is no "happily ever after" for your family if your parents divorce. But there can be a new kind of life that includes your mom, your dad, and you. As you begin that life, try to remember these things.

○ Don't listen to people who want to blame someone for your parents' divorce. No matter what they have done, your mom and dad will always be your mom and dad. Try to forgive them.

○ Your parents' divorce was between them. It was not your fault.

A divorce does not change the love between parents and children.

**The most important thing to
remember is this:
You are not alone.**

○ Don't take one parent's side against the other.
Try to stay out of any fights that happen
between your parents.

○ Your parents love you. They may seem angry at
you. They may seem to want to spend time by
themselves. But they do love you.

○ Your parents need your love. Show them how
much you love them. But be careful to have
your own life too.

○ Let go of the past. Your parents' marriage is
over. You need to accept that.

○ Your parents have a new life to live too. They
may date and even remarry some day.

The most important thing for you to remember
is this: You are not alone. There are many people
who understand what has happened to you. Those
people want to help you. Talk to them.

Glossary—*Explaining New Words*

child support Money the supporting parent must pay to the other after a divorce. The money is used to help pay for the childrens' food, clothes, and other expenses.

clergyman A minister, priest, or rabbi .

custody Care and control over children after a divorce. Joint custody means that both parents must care for the children and make decisions about them.

depressed Very sad. If you are just a little depressed, you might say that you feel "down." If you are very depressed, you may need to see a doctor for help.

suicide The act of taking your life (killing yourself) on purpose.

support group People who have problems that are alike and who get together to help each other.

violent Excited, usually in anger, so that you lose control. A storm that causes a lot of damage is called a violent storm. A person who is violent may try to harm someone nearby.

visitation rights Rules about how often and when parents who do not live with children may see them. These rights are usually written down by a judge at the time of a divorce.

Where To Get Help

If you feel down, you should talk to an adult you trust. That person might be a teacher, a counselor, a clergyman or someone in your family. But there are times when you may need special help. You may feel that you want to die. Or you may feel that you want to run away from home.

If you feel this way, look in the Yellow Pages of your phone book. Look for the words CRISIS CENTER or MENTAL HEALTH CENTER. Or call your local hospital's emergency room. Someone there may be able to help.

If you feel as if you want to die, or you think one of your parents may commit suicide, there is another way to find help. Call 1-800-555-1212. Ask the operator for the number of a SUICIDE HOTLINE. The operator will give you another number to call that begins with 1-800. (There is no charge for calling ''800'' numbers.)

If one of your parents harms you or tries to harm you, call the National Child Abuse Hotline, 1-800-333-7233.

For Further Reading

Fayerweather Street School, The Unit. Rofer, Eric
   E., ed. *The Kids' Book of Divorce.* Lexington,
   Mass.: The Lewis Publishing Co., 1981, 123
   pages. This book was put together by 20
   students, ages 11 to 14. They talk about how and
   why divorce happens and give ideas about how
   to feel better after a divorce.

Krementz, Jill. *How It Feels When Parents Divorce.*
   New York: Alfred A. Knopf, 1984, 115 pages.
   In this book, young people from age 7 to 16
   share their feelings about their parents' divorces.

Mann, Peggy. *My Dad Lives in a Downtown Hotel.* Garden City, New York: Doubleday & Company, Inc., 96 pages. *(Fiction)* This is a story about a boy named Joey. He becomes closer to his father after his parents get a divorce.

Okimoto, Jean Davies. *My Mother Is Not Married to My Father.* New York: G.P. Putnam's Sons, 1981, 109 pages. *(Fiction)* This story is told by a girl named Cynthia. Her parents are divorced, and she doesn't like her dad's girlfriend.

Sobol, Harriet Langsam. *My Other-Mother, My Other-Father.* New York: Macmillan Publishing Co., Inc., 1979, 34 pages. This book is about a girl whose divorced parents marry other people.

Stenson, Janet Sinberg. *Now I have a Stepparent and it's kind of confusing.* New York: Avon Books, 1979, 36 pages. This book is about a boy whose mother marries again after a divorce.

Index

About the Author
Linda Carlson Johnson taught junior high and high school English for
nine years before embarking on a second career in publishing. After
reporting for daily and weekly newspapers, she became an editor at
Field Publications in Middletown, Connecticut. There, she has written
for *Weekly Reader*, the children's newspaper, and *Know Your World
Extra*, a special education periodical for junior high students. Currently,
Ms. Johnson is editing family publications for Field.

About the Editor
Evan Stark is a well-known sociologist, educator, and therapist
as well as a popular lecturer on women's and children's health issues.
Dr. Stark was the Henry Rutgers Fellow at Rutgers University, an as-
sociate at the Institution for Social and Policy Studies at Yale University, and a Fulbright Fellow at the University of Essex. He is the author
of many publications in the field of family relations and is the father of
four children.

Acknowledgments and Photo Credits

Photographs by Stuart Rabinowitz

Design/Production: Blackbirch Graphics, Inc.
Cover Photograph: Stuart Rabinowitz